I am Barry MacDonald. I received the *dharma* name *Tekkan*, which means "Iron Man," a settled practitioner of great determination.

Copyright © 2022 Tekkan
Artwork Copyright © 2022

All rights reserved.
First Printing, 2022
ISBN 979-8-9867262-0-5

To contact Tekkan please email:
buddhaboy1289@gmail.com

This book is dedicated to my marvelous artists. The wild horses gracing this book were painted by Will Ersland. The other paintings were done by my daughter, Jocelyn Figueroa.

Table of Contents

Jackson Pollack Villanelle . . . . Page 37

Second Thoughts Villanelle . . . . . . Page 54

A Pompous Sestina . . . . .Page 78

A Gossipy Sestina . . . . .Page 80

Flighty Terza Rima . . . . .Page 93

Sour Grapes Terza Rima . . . . Page 94

The Lombardi Trophy Sestina. . . . Page 95

Everyday Mind XXVIII

I come to my window to play
on a cloudy or sunny day

I like to explore while quiet
it's helpful to linger for a bit

I fish in the air for the words
they are transient like the birds

I sit at my desk on my chair
I am hunting for insights to share

I have come to love wordy play
it is the simple joy of my day.

One has to be quiet to hear it
it helps to be gentle to love it

the sound is a gift of the season
and it serves no purposeful reason

its flow is a balm to a spirit
it's the breeze in the leaves that weaves it

the wind in the trees is beautiful
listening quietly is restful.

This year the winter seemed to drag
on forever with such a lag

between my *expectations* and
springtime *resurrection* and

I could have complained to the wind
which would only have served to wound

my spirit with *frustration* so
I let my *celebration* go

until the time of fruition
of natural exhibition —

today my roses are blooming
a warm empty sky is glowing

I approach very close to sniff
and breathe in a delicious whiff

of rose scent and then I notice
the summer metamorphosis

of the scattering rose petals
delicately pink and settled

on concrete on my patio
as the bush is letting them go.

The empty sky is ablaze
which imparts in me a daze

as I *gaze* at the valley —
for an hour I tally

the different forms of birds
I don't know all of the words

there are the herons and geese —
I see the wind doesn't cease

by the labor of their flight
which demands the utmost might

of the feathery creatures —
I see it is a feature

of the vastness of the sky
swallowing birds as they fly.

If I were a squirrel the cottonwood
in the yard of my property would *be*
the end of the world and I'd resemble
explorers in sailing ships trespassing
across dangerous boundaries tempting
fate and possibly paying the price by
tipping and plunging into the abyss.

If I were a squirrel would the sunlight
at the tiptop of the cottonwood *be*
a temptation to *me* — would I hunger
to know what it's like to clamber onto
the slenderest twig at the utmost point
where the leaves turning and sparking in the
light would become the *empyrean sky?*

Is it a tug of *liberation* to
probe the edge of the knowable — or is
it an *obsessional maladjustment*
to life propelling our *restlessness?*

What does the cottonwood mean to me?
it's a towering hulk of a tree

once its roots did break my sewage pipe
which is plenty of reason to gripe

I see it standing every season
I think it's a worthy paragon

it's the opposite of symmetry
it is a burly grotesquery

it's no end of trouble I believe
when it drops a mass of yellow leaves

it's a burst of creativity —
clue to nature's *spontaneity*.

The thing about everyday mind is that
there are patterns a mind naturally
spins of a repetitive quality
which tend not to rise to a level of
conscious awareness for the person who
is creating the thoughts so that the course
of a life resembles the scampering
of a mouse inside a maze that has been
designed by the mouse itself — *it is my
intention — gentle reader — to plumb
the pregnancy of each moment using
the solitude that I enjoy to watch
the currents of my mind and encourage
those patterns that nurture relaxation.*

A trick of life — which can be thought of as
spiritual jujitsu — is to be poised
enough so as to be genuinely
spontaneous and thus to act with a
consequence summoning *liberation.*

I've freed myself from the idea that
it's necessary to count syllables
and measure the length of my lines because
I've done a dump truck load of that reaching
a point of exhaustion so now I'd like
to fiddle with prose poetry which is
not defined by anyone I know of
because it's hard to determine the *pith*
of poetry once conventions are stripped
away and I'm finding that I like to
rhyme some of the *time* while attending to
the throbbing of the strong beats within my
lines which gives a plucky emphasis to
the meaning of words — *which may be important.*

It's curious that years of
doing poetry has left
proclivities disposing
me to compose insights in
predictable patterns from
which I seek liberation.

The intellect is subservient to
emotion so I find myself spinning
the same sad tales of woe inside of my
cranium even as I know the toll
that bankrupt justifications exact
from my spirit even as I lie in
bed consciously aware I'm squandering
precious energy in useless mental
confabulations as I recognize
I can't effectively stand guard against
the next disturbing thought that *pops* within
my head but that I am responsible
for resisting the compulsive allure
of the runaway *silly* narratives.

Ignorance and fear
and lust are hydra-
headed maladies
that only the gift
of *relaxation*
can cure.

Without bridle
or a saddle

or stirrups
my thoughts disrupt

my tranquility
at three

a.m. —
I am

a head with a bowl
containing a soul

of wild mustangs.

Summer

        cavorts

     dragonflies

                    with eyes of 60,000 lenses

        turning sunlight

incandescent.

One does wonder where things are going as
radio telescopes are confirming
scientific insights into the big
bang signified by the sight of a haze
of radiation originating
in a trillionth slice of a second and
with trillions of degrees of heat which has
been expanding from the humble size of
the period that ends this poem to
a seeming infinity of space for
14 billion years as meanwhile every
moment in each direction possesses
a wealth of unearthly forms surpassing
the imagination of any mind.

The bee hummingbird is
native to the Cuban
archipelago and
it pollinates more than
1,500
flowers within a day.

I do need a spark of insight to launch
a poem and I accept the task of
finding an ending with *panache* and there
is the choice of RhymeZone.com which helps
to settle on a suitable array
of possible words but nothing happens
unless I'm able to linger in the
midst of the pregnancy of emptiness
that of itself without much effort of
my will — apart from keeping an open
mind — *spontaneously* assembles the
happy connections putting good words in
proper order — once I manage how to
sit with an empty head *I love it.*

Once the habit of
coming to my desk
and window is fixed
a question arises —
*what is the pith of
spontaneity?*

Jane can't *abstain*

from pinging our meditation group
with oddball intellectual loops

and today she brought to our attention
a crazy phenomenon she mentioned —

immortal jellyfish —
I'm sure I wouldn't wish

to be alive forever
dealing with whatever

it is a jellyfish thinks
because I think it would stink.

An empty head is a heavenly gift
I don't have to think about anything
I am not sorry befuddled or miffed

a natural absence creates a lift
too many arguments come with a sting
an empty head is a heavenly gift

I like the quiet solitude to sift
an open repose is helpful to sing
I am not sorry befuddled or miffed

a mind is always liable to drift
a mind is obsessive crazy and clings
an empty head is a heavenly gift

a disturbing notion is very swift
it constructs of itself a painful string
I am not sorry befuddled or miffed

from emptiness I have the chance to shift
and then my *happiness* comes with a *zing*
an empty head is a heavenly gift
I am not sorry befuddled or miffed.

I am aware that I declared myself
to be liberated from having to
count syllables and thus measuring the
length of my *lines* and that it's no longer
necessary for me to fix *rhymes* at
the end of my *lines* and that I am now
willing to experiment with offbeat
patterns of words and yet I do find that
I am relapsing into poems of
14 lines of 10 syllables a *line*
which is a sonnet without *rhyme* so all
I can say is that just because I said that
I "*don't have to*" doesn't mean that sometimes —
if lazy — *I might very much want to.*

I am like a drunk
returning to drink

he doesn't think about it
he exuberates in it

my style is just a habit —
I am a thoughtless rabbit.

My closed eyes are facing the sun
I'm savoring a haze of heat

I'm composing some rhymes for fun
who cares if I happen to cheat?

the sun is impossibly bright
my eyes continuously see

my closed eyelids are very light
they look the brightest red to me.

A portion of the branches of both of
the apple trees by my driveway have been
withering and the bark on one of them
is separating from the trunk even
as I see that they are sprouting the forms
of incipient apples on branches
untouched by infestation — I have had
such fun watching my apple trees since I
bought them as saplings at Fleet Farm when my
children were very young and now they've left
home and have graduated from college
while my wife and I divorced years ago
and I am adjusting myself to a
life of solitude teaching transience.

I feel responsible
for their welfare thinking
that I should *do something*
but my ecologist
friend Jason says it is
better to buy new trees.

I remember a January day
when the temperature was far below
zero and colder than it had been for
many decades to be followed on the
next day by a thaw and a shower of
rain while I was leaving home and looking
left in my car seeing the hundreds of
drops of water hanging from the crooks of
my apple trees refracting the sunlight
resulting from the clearing of the sky
as I was *gobsmacked* by the loveliness
of the sight set amid the whiplash of
circumstances including the sudden
mushiness of snow smearing all the cars.

It is not one thing
that's liable to
transform all of a
sudden but there's a
cascade of events.

As for me I'm going to tweak the meaning
of "free verse" to liberate myself from
the notion that I "have to" follow the
conventions of any form after I
proved that I can do the Houdini trick
of rhyming sonnets and instead I will
be promoting a stream of consciousness
allowing the words themselves as they fall
into place to show me how poetry
should be composed today and rhythm and
rhyme and counting syllables are part of
the play of words but the exploration
of the phenomenal world remains the
pith of the *point* of my *poetizing*.

I don't know how it
feels to you but for
me poems longer
than 14 lines are
hard to focus on.

I am a proud Minnesotan who lacks
the resources to move somewhere else *so*
I traipse through the winters as well as I
might and in the park yesterday in a
maple tree I spied a clump of yellow
leaves at the end of June reminding me
that daylight is shrinking and that autumn
is coming as I've borne many seasons
knowing February cold penetrates
to the brain stem with a frost settling on
the synapses eventually with
age and as for me I've developed a
syndrome — *Post Traumatic February
Disorder* — with symptomatic sarcasm.

The leaves do last
a little longer
than the bloom of
the petals of
flowers but not
so much longer.

Even identical twins who mirror
each other's pattern of chemistry will
diverge in their personalities and
they acquire varied likes and dislikes
that harden over time into habits
separating them into contrasting
paths through life so even if together
they experience the same event they
taste it from different angles coming
away with mismatched memories enough
to show that each of us contributes to
the cosmos a unique perspective with
a sum beyond comprehension as we
juggle and *jangle* to communicate.

Words on paper
have a certain
fixity but
the tasting of
the *pith* of the
meaning varies.

The apple trees and lilacs
delight me in the spring
as they *fling* their blooming
scent to the winds blowing
the petals away for
a cycle of seasons.

Roses and peonies
coincide in early
summer by blossoming
and approximating
the solstice of the *bloom*
of the peak of sunlight.

One of the alluring messages I
heard on entering the groups that foster
recovery from alcoholism
is that I don't have to live as if life
were a contest of wills where it's up to
me to wrest love and satisfaction for
myself in competition with others
and instead of being in collision
with people I could dissipate trouble
by turning frustration over to a
higher power that need not be defined
to be relied on with the faith that no
matter what happens *I'll be OK*—
which to you may sound very *simplistic*.

I've lived this faith
almost forty
years growing roots
into something
I don't define.

A group of people with the purpose of
being sober without mind-distorting
chemicals is effective as long as
balancing is the focus as I have
found that isolation fosters fear but
the strength of heartful communication
coupled with the group experience of
using principles of sobriety
is enough to instill strength and hope in
a wretch of a drunk or an addict who
lacks the relaxing optimism of
knowledgable companions as each of
us fashions our own connection to a
higher power that suits us where we are.

We meet apart from
compulsive noisy
concatenation
called society.

I relish the sight of a summer rose
I needn't worry about anything
with my sandals I liberate my toes

I seize the day and minimize my clothes
exuberant sunshine comes with a zing
I relish the sight of a summer rose

I sit within heat and so often doze
once in a while a memory will sting
with my sandals I liberate my toes

in July and August my toes aren't froze
I recall the past but don't have to cling
I relish the sight of a summer rose

the scent of a rose does tickle my nose
the bush surrenders petals with a fling
with my sandals I liberate my toes

with effortless brilliance the summer flows
the seasons transform in a ceaseless ring
I relish the sight of a summer rose
with my sandals I liberate my toes.

Even though I'm 64 years old I
find myself leaner and speedier with
each passing season as I'm pedaling
my bicycle relaxed and sweating and
drinking in the distance with my eyes and
rising off the seat and sprinting up the
slope to Houlton which is not the ordeal
that it was a summer ago as I
am becoming intimate with my route
knowing how to jerk my body upward
with my arms and back to avoid the bump
of mismatched concrete that otherwise would
jar my front tire and me and my greatest
test is the wild and variable wind.

It is sad to see at the
furthest extent of my route
on the highest slope all of
the fledgling cottonwoods that
won't slip the county mower.

Purple thistles emerged
by the way on the highest slope

I mark them as I surge —
on my bicycle — *who could be a mope*

out in the sun satisfying an urge
for frivolous speed *in a lope*

of easy motion? summer is a splurge
of sensations as I see and hear on the slope

at the top a troop of red-winged blackbirds —
they are a *spice* for my summer words.

The shadow of the
bicycle and me angles —
swallows wheel and swoop.

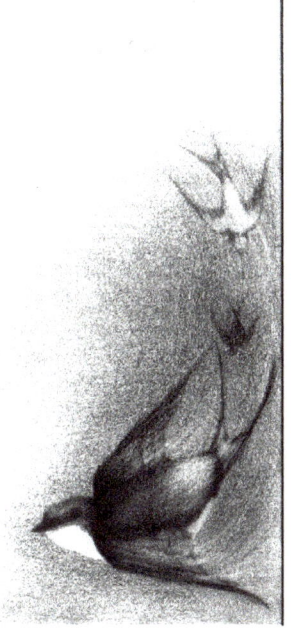

*I am suspicious that I'm stuck with my
habits* while there are insights and marvels
around the corners of the limits of
what I'm able to see — and there are hints
within the language and gestures I catch
from others that suggest they are just as
confused and dissatisfied as I am
striving for something better over the
horizon of awareness — I believe
that together — *however different
we appear on the surface* — most of us
are not sufficiently gratified where
we are and — but for the lack of *some thing*
we *don't have* — *we could be liberated.*

I stir the bowl of my mind
with morning meditation
recipes of poetic
forms and the *spice* of words and
yet I bump hinderances.

From my earliest taste of the *dharma*
reading *Siddhartha* as a teenager
a stubborn core of me was repulsed by
the self-negation proffered as the cure
to suffering as I felt a lack of
love and couldn't stanch a hunger for a
basking in the adoration of a
beloved as I was mired in a
Western world of endless competition
but I found enchantment inside the words
we are what we think — with our thoughts we make
the world — to speak and act with an impure
mind is to make troubles follow as the
wheels that follow a cart drawn by an ox.

Speak and act with a pure
mind and happiness
follows like a shadow.

I appreciate the drift
of clouds necessitating
repose to see while sitting
in Pioneer Park at dawn.

I am drawn to glimpses of
the shadow of me on a
bicycle cascading as
a nimble apparition.

How easy it is with words to dabble
with scientific theories about the
bang that erupted from *nothing* — when space
did not exist and *inside* and *outside*
wasn't possible beforehand — and how
pleasant it is to speculate on the
eventual dissipation of the
heat of energy binding the cosmos
together when the *quarks* will cease spinning
and everything will disintegrate and
nothing will return — and how wonderful
it is to slice a moment into a
trillion parts proclaiming *picoseconds*
to measure each comic phenomenon.

For me the question of the
predominating silence
existing outside of
atmospheres like the Earth's
is the eeriest thing.

My beard is a force that continues to grow
It's a hint that I am partly animal

which needn't imply that I'm irrational
perhaps it's left over from living with snow

it's true my ancestors had hair all over
except for the hands and the bottoms of feet

which could be a blessing with shivering sleet
how propitious to be warm all over

why are our women without hairy faces?
they do display the *intelligent* passions

they are the experts of subtle emotions
where would we be without feminine graces?

are my bristles a tinge of the barbarous?
do I tend on occasion to be a brute?

I am an animal who puts on a suit
my grasp of elegance is precarious.

Jackson Pollack Villanelle

Oh to be famous by dribbling with paint
a sweep of a wrist produces a swirl
to be a creator without a taint

to play for a living lacking restraint
dabbling with crimson and making a curl
oh to be famous by dribbling with paint

it's probably true that no one's a saint
with a twirl of a wrist to trace a pearl
to be a creator without a taint

having a style that's especially quaint
to be impetuous and whirl and hurl
oh to be famous by dribbling with paint

it seems lackadaisical but it ain't
a canvas engenders a cosmic whorl
to be a creator without a taint

interlacing colors beyond constraint
to saturate a brush and then to twirl
oh to be famous by dribbling with paint
to be a creator without a taint.

Each drop and dribble are a trace of motion

the sweep of an arm and wrist is on canvas

was there joy in the mixing of colors?

does chaos escape pattern?

is it purposeless?

promiscuous?

what does your eye see?

which emotion?

It's a fact that the iron composed in
our bodies originated from a
supernova of a much more massive
sun than our own as our sun doesn't have
the crushing gravity sufficient to
conjure iron so that without a far
distant cataclysmic eruption in
the silence of space breathing heart pumping
life on Earth wouldn't exist and human
minds are capable of tracing just so
much of the labyrinthine mysteries but
beyond our comprehension lies a point
of stupefaction even for our
cleverest mathematical geniuses.

Can I be happy when events
seem to be opposed to my well-
being and can I muster
the faith that I will be OK
no matter what eventuates?

Jackson Pollack doesn't impress as a
mathematical savant but he was an
artist with a knack with dribbles and drops
of paint for verisimilitude who
with chaotic and kaleidoscopic
verve created poignant portraits of what
seem to me to be moments of cosmic
inspiration and eruption within
the eerie silence of space and yet with
the motion of his wrist and arm wasn't
there inherent pattern underlying
art and even as he tried he couldn't
escape the bonds of the physics of the
way things are — *and so he could only play.*

Jackson explored the realms
of the unconscious
but couldn't evade
alcoholism.

What kind of mind applies a measure as
exacting as a *picosecond* which
is a *trillionth* of a second to the
pulse of the cutting of a laser beam?

how much further can a society
penetrate into the subtleties of
the cosmos without having mastered a
grasp of compassion and benevolence?

how exquisite is the balancing of
the thrusting accumulation of
technology with our capacity
for mass *hypnosis* and *barbarity* —

it's worthwhile to be mindful — *extinction*
is a part of the *play* of the cosmos.

It's good that we lost a sense
of the inevitable
progress of humanity —
there's opportunity for
humble curiosity.

I sit with companions for an hour of talk
I balance the gab with a view of the sky

it's hard to escape the demands of the clock
I watch the flutter of a white butterfly

I manage to follow the meaning of words
I am bored and restless and hungry for lunch

I lighten my mind with the gambol of birds
in the middle of chatter I have a hunch

something is unfolding in the moment now
clouds are transforming at a daydreaming pace

I'm imbibing a taste of the Chinese *Tao*
sights are disappearing not leaving a trace

there's churning magic in every direction
a thousand events are transpiring here

a mind delights in a choice of selection
vibrant vibrations with sensations cohere.

Gentle reader I've been asked to explain
why it is I'm moved to assemble words
on paper whether I'm seeking praise for
ego gratification or I have
an urge for gathering companions whom
I'll never meet to accompany me
trudging on the path to liberation
and I don't know what causes me to take
the pains I do weaving webs of one-
way communication — but there is an
oddball inducement in the challenge that
in my imagination *I see you
and I want to grasp ahold of your mind
and compel you to follow to the end.*

*Can I entice you to
appreciate the play
of sound and syllables
in a string of words to
trace with your eyes the
traipsing turning of lines?*

I wonder whether it's possible to
compose a one-word poem that's missing
even the context of a title but
I am sure when I put one word beside
another of necessity the weight
of a culture comes into play with the
conventions of grammar and in English
there is the patter of resonant and
wimpy syllables making a rhythm
woven with the meaning inherent in
the sounds we make with our *tongues* and I think
it's pleasing to employ a tasteful sense
of symmetry so that's reason enough
for me to measure the length of my lines.

Plop

It's easy to daydream and dispense with time
summer's muggy and is making me lazy

afternoon is a boon — *my thoughts are hazy* —
but then I'm struck and pirouette on a dime

it sprang with the impulse of a lightning bolt
just as my acuity was at an ebb

I listlessly ambled to a spider's web
a sticky encumbrance imparted a jolt

it is hot as it wraps and clings to my face
quite sneaky and nasty and surpassing weird

the net is dexterous and clutches my beard
I swipe with my hands at the devilish lace

I think of the critter that's lying in wait
such a disgusting bug with an appetite

so clever and patient and ready to bite
how delightfully magnificent it ain't.

How odd people are as traditions change
As the wheeled cannon that graces the top
of the hill above the valley beside
the historic courthouse symbolizes
as the steel of the Civil War machine
is coated with a thick layer of black
paint impervious to weather looking
harmless as the glances of passersby
hardly notice yet there it remains as
a reminder that once the honor of
men demanded their assembly into
lines marching toward the enemy assailed
by mini balls cannon balls grapeshot that
shredded their organs and splintered their bones.

Today children sleeping in
their beds playing in their back
yards in Chicago are killed
by bullets haphazardly
aimed by rival gangs and the
newspapers barely notice.

The Red Spot

The *Tao* the Chinese explored extends
in every direction and yet cannot
be grasped as everything is included
cycles within cycles going who knows
where involving even the Red Spot on
Jupiter of winds of hundreds of miles
per hour howling as a hurricane as
seen from Earth for more than a century
a curiosity coexisting
as another detail of the moment
as a clue for questions about pattern
and anomaly about emptiness
and form and how funny it is to note
a similarity with my thinking.

Nonsensical
rubbish
cyclones
of thought
persist.

Some thoughts are like weeds with roots infecting
the psyche arising randomly as
when I stumbled on an ad on Facebook
soliciting submissions of poems
for publication — *which I did* — only
to be tricked to subscribe — *which I did* — with
a credit card discovering later
a charge of $12 dollars was being made
weekly inducing panic and outrage
impelling me to a website where my
password was denied my email address
unrecognized spurring a phone call to
my credit card provider whereupon
we canceled my card to restore order.

The card representative
said fraud may be reported
but authorized vendors can't
be denied leaving me in
limbo.

My ecologist friend burst a notion
of mine that the birds were similar to
jazz musicians on spontaneous riffs
of inspiration when he remarked that
each species sings its pattern and can't so
much indulgently improvise and yet
today Fran intoned that there are mimics
such as the brown thrashers mockingbirds and
gray catbirds liberated enough to
play and different species select a
varied tune in the morning and evening
and so the birds enjoy an intermix
of habit and compulsion along with
a curious degree of discretion.

A poet has a wider
array of discretion but
remains bound by compulsion
habit and rubbishy thoughts.

From the clouds in the sky the rain will drop
the drops on a lake perpetuate rills
a frog and a pond occasion a *plop*

the blooms of peonies so often droop
blusters make music with leaves on the hills
from the clouds in the sky the rain will drop

the swallows by the river wheel and swoop
the air in the morning quite often chills
a frog and a pond occasion a *plop*

a squirrel on a maple climbs to the top
on the verge of the rain the air is still
from the clouds in the sky the rain will drop

the leaves of a willow will flow and droop
lying on the lawn is a pigeon's quill
a frog and a pond occasion a *plop*

a drop on the brim of my hat goes bop
the summer is filled with brilliance and thrills
from the clouds in the sky the rain will drop
a frog and a pond occasion a *plop*.

Are
you a
person who
attends to whether
there are unnecessary words
lazily composed within the lines of
poetry who quibbles with the selections
of the poet who is only mindful of filling
out the prescribed number of syllables to
satisfy the dictates of a form whereas you
have given time and energy to open this
book when you could be watching the
television informing yourself of the
peccadillos of the politicians
in Washington D.C. but
instead you're reading
a glop of words—
yes?

I don't know how one does prose poetry
without measuring and finagling the
lengths of lines and sounds of words which must be
sinewy without fatty verbiage
that fuzzes the clarity of the piece
as I believe what distinguishes verse
from prose is the *integrity* of lines
crafted with an *eye* and *ear* for impact
easily absorbed when listening or
reading without *higgledy-piggledy*
phrases on a page careless of the right
margin so sloppy beyond redemption —
I would rather train my words to hop on
platforms and roar like lions and tigers.

You won't catch me
lathering on
phrases in an
amorphous mess.

Second Thoughts Villanelle

Remember you and I we had our chat
you heard but you didn't listen to me
I told you it wouldn't happen like that

you are humble now that your plans fell flat
all you can do is to clear the debris
remember you and I we had our chat

it's always better to avoid a spat
I believe you've earned your anxiety
I told you it wouldn't happen like that

you've shown your absurdity with éclat
it's wise not to parade hypocrisy
remember you and I we had our chat

I suppose by now you feel like a gnat
your shame is approaching its apogee
I told you it wouldn't happen like that

you've never played the quiet diplomat
things could have been smoother — *don't you agree?*
remember you and I we had our chat
I told you it wouldn't happen like that.

where's the guttural
cacophony of crows?
here are the grackles.

The roots and stems and leaves of roses and
peonies remain but the blooms passed a
month ago — the cacophony of birds
at dawn is lessened as territories
are marked — the lustrous green of the pristine
leaves of spring is dulled and insects nibble
holes — my ear is inured to the sigh of
breeze in the leaves as the contrast with the
leafless wind of winter isn't fresh — the
heat of afternoon is languorous and
sticky sapping energy — it takes an
effort of will to ride my bike and yet
I know on a distant slope a red-winged
blackbird is perching on a sign — *thrilling*.

Through an open window
at dawn as incense smoke
curls a solitary
dove *glorifies*
summer.

Just as the James Webb telescope offers
mesmerizing photos of the cosmos
as it was billions of years ago as
a sparkling nebulae of jewels birthing
trillions and trillions of galaxies in
a pinpoint of space as seen from the Earth
an ideology is infecting
the nations of Earth as a coterie
of elite is determined to control
technology justice education
commerce energy and history with
the ethos the masses will own nothing
and be happy about it as they *play*
their *game* of relentless accusation.

News media narratives
are crafted to hook the hearts
with volatile emotion
to fashion the approved truths
and to castigate *wrongthink*.

In a corner of my mind there is a
tinge of guilt of a memory of how
my mother used to wash the dishes by
filling the sink with warm water and by
dropping only a *dollop* of dish soap
in the water which was the minimum
amount of soap sufficient for the job
as she lived through the Great Depression and
thrift is a habit imbued so that a
bottle of liquid soap would last a while
and she didn't think about what she did
while I am neither wealthy nor careful
in my consumption and so I fritter
goods away as a thoughtless *profligate*.

Mom is also
in the habit
of not throwing
things away which
is a *nuisance*.

After summer solstice
the sun scorches afternoon
and we anticipate the
dog days of August

after winter solstice
comes the burden of the
bite of January
and February cold

the temporary and
temperate days of the
equinox pass by as
a tonic for the skin.

It's not me riding a bicycle in
the afternoon — *it is only my body* —
it's not me reading the politics of
the day on the internet dividing
society into bullies allies
and the naïve — *it is only my mind* —
I'm not sure it's me who rises early
from bed drinks coffee and writes poetry
leveraging morning transparency
to offset the negativity of
politics as I suspect it's only
the path of my habits running along
as I wonder — *who am I* — apart from
the choices I make within ignorance?

The shadow of me
on a bicycle
epitomizes
plump potential.

My fingers tap the keyboard and my eyes
attend to the kaleidoscopic vibes
emanating from the monitor of
my computer and I have hours to roam
within cyber reality as I
rely on intellectual constructs
painstakingly accumulated that
reinforce opinions and direct me
to the patterns I'm *sure* are correct so
that I am capable of having the
conversations and writing the essays
necessary to do my job and how
difficult it is not to collide with
people who don't see things the way I do.

My ears absorb
propitious
conversation
making way for
changes of heart.

Finding the posture of mind to come to
decisions about the welfare of Mom —
who absently leaves the water running
at the faucet — who on the way to the
grocery store with her daughter forgets
where she's going — balancing opinions
among siblings about whether it's safe
to leave her alone at home where she could
fall and be left for hours — summoning
thought about taking her from the comfort
of *home* with the kitchen dining living
bed rooms — *where her children grew* — the porch the
grand piano and the dozens of house-
plants that she tends *isn't pleasant duty.*

My sister her daughter
is a force confronting
my brother and me with
facts I don't want to see.

Accumulating dust
covers the thousands of
things that mean so much
and it becomes a sad and
intimidating task
to displace a parent's
heart.

Politicians

When he is lying it is hard to stop
to play the angles it helps to be sly
if she is exposed then her polls will drop

after a while integrity goes "pop"
slippery phrases are useful for lies
when he is lying it is hard to stop

it's easy to think the voters are dopes
a shift of position comes on the fly
if she is exposed then her polls will drop

the trust of the public is sure to droop
the facts and the truth are best *classified*
when he is lying it is hard to stop

the news narratives perpetuate poop
nefarious motives are well disguised
if she is exposed then her polls will drop

may we rely on his honesty? nope
in her heart she thinks she is justified
when he is lying it is hard to stop
if she is exposed then her polls will drop.

Masses of people are easily fooled
it's fear and anger that motivates mobs
our politicians are cleverly schooled

accusing narratives are often sold
casting the blame is the media's job
masses of people are easily fooled

the nuance of details isn't told
intellect is cold but emotions throb
our politicians are cleverly schooled

the same techniques are repeatedly spooled
the scope of complexity is a blob
masses of people are easily fooled

our jealousies and resentments are tooled
crafting the slogans is an inside job
our politicians are cleverly schooled

dissimulation sings as it is bold
our slippery politicos are snobs
masses of people are easily fooled
our politicians are cleverly schooled.

Does the frog
or the pond
go — *plop* — ?

both the pond
and the frog
ripple
water
and air.

Dear reader it may appear to you that
I am egregiously critical of
those who assume the duties of public
service in the marbled palaces of
the nation's and the states' capitols and
that I castigate every one as if
all were of a dubious character
unworthy of trust — *but such is not my
opinion* — as there are some without the
self-aggrandizing impulse who act on
principle — and if this weren't true then the
prosperity of America would
be much lower than it is — the *tricky*
task is to distinguish the *trustworthy*.

Persisting attention
to the details and
the nuances of the
policies over time
reveals very much.

Poetry for me is a frolicsome
play of words and I want to deserve your
attention and as life isn't always
*moonligh*t and *butterflies* I like to spice
and fortify my offerings with a
slap of reality with a *dollop*
of appropriate *cynicism* for
the princes and queens who rule us without
becoming a partisan myself so
that you could whimsically follow and
chuckle with the words agreeing just so
much as to suppose I am describing
what you believe from the opposite side —
*and if I can do that anger dissolve*s.

As long as people are
not jailed because of
their opinions there is
room for hilarity.

Overstimulation is a problem
of modern life as there is always a
shooting or a hurricane or a war
in the distance seizing the attention
of the masses added to the tension
of paying the mortgage educating
children doing a job which is apart
from the Chinese Zen temples centuries
ago where the Japanese monk Dogen
learned his tricks where with a fierce clarity
of meditation he discovered the
eyes are horizontal and the nose
is vertical which is a cynosure
with which to eliminate distraction.

A calm persisting
awareness of mind
with *energy* may
strip away the noise
with *simplicity*.

Buddhists have a way of pointing to the
emptiness that gives birth to the eyes and
ears and tongue and nose and skin and the mind
holding the world and assuming likes and
dislikes making decisions creating
opinions elaborating theories
of roles and duties and expectations
of how things should be with a direction
liable to frustration — *certain of
death* — with all of it heaped upon a *void*
of incomprehensible nothing as
who among us remembers being born
who experiences going to sleep
and never waking up — *who wants to know?*

Stripping away
everything one
holds dear there is
no ground below
no sky above.

The Buddhists are *peculiar* characters
asserting that words can only point in
the direction of liberation but
are useless in seizing liberation
suggesting it comes accidentally
somehow allowing me to *goof off* while
meditating making an oval of
my hands imagining that my thoughts and
being emanate from the space within
my fingers and palms which are resting on
my lap and the emptiness *vibrates* with
energy and I feel the tension of
my spine and the relaxation of my
shoulders from the *locus* within my hands.

I am *lounging*
about playing
mind games waiting
innocently
for the *lightning*.

If a frog and
a pond go

plop

in the forest
is there a *sound?*

without
an ear
there is
vibration
but no
sound.

Thirty-one years ago today about
9 p.m. in Kyoto Japan a nurse
burst into a room of a hospital
with my newly birthed son Joshua who
had a red face and a curiously
pointy head due to the force of pushing
against the narrow constriction of the
birth canal and as I held my first child
in my arms it was a moment unlike
any other of an immensity
that cannot be relived accurately
in memory except to say that I
knew that life would be different from then
on as I had *responsibilities*.

The ordeal of birth
pinched his little head
and his *flaming* face
cried in discomfort.

A wisp of a cloud transforms in the light
there isn't a haze in the air today
the strength of the sun is supremely bright

the sun on the clouds is a pristine white
there is just a tinge of a shade of gray
a wisp of a cloud transforms in the light

the clouds in the sky are a blissful sight
the sun is ascending holding sway
the strength of the sun is supremely bright

the drift of clouds is a feathery sight
the wind from the north is flowing away
a wisp of a cloud transforms in the light

I take the time for a moment's delight
the pace of the clouds pacifies a day
the strength of the sun is supremely bright

what a change this is from the deep of night
not a curl of a cloud may go astray
a wisp of a cloud transforms in the light
the strength of the sun is supremely bright

The sun makes
my closed eyelids
red

from the pressure
of the heat
on the skin
of my forehead

I know where
the sun
is.

When the trials of adversity begin
to bite elemental fear arises
and I think it's up to me to balance
and step carefully against hostile winds
as if I were walking a tightrope and
a moment's inattention would topple
me into the abyss as within there's
the whisper I am separate and lost
but I also know the impulse of fear
is a lie and I have only to join the
fellowship of recovered drunks to feel
again the balm of peace founded on the
shared practice and experience of the
art of letting go and relaxation.

I can't wrench myself
into a better
way of thinking
and feeling — I have
to *surf* emotion.

Messages of peace permeate human
communication once the ears are trained
to hear and the heart is opened as I
remember the example and words of
a Zen master in a temple as he
raised a staff and struck the tatami and
said *"with wholehearted practice you cannot
miss"* which I take to mean liberation
is like the ground beneath our feet and we
need only to relax and let things be
without inflaming emotions and then
delusions will dissolve and myriad
particles will bear testimony that
the perfection of things is without taint.

This is a message
I have yet to learn
as I journey to
arrive at just where the
Earth supports my feet.

A Pompous Sestina

Do you suppose most poets are lazy?
is it true they don't have enough to do?
as they lose themselves by watching the clouds?
poets practice an oddball industry
they depend upon curiosity
their common failing is pomposity

even a clown displays pomposity
he's not serious but mostly lazy
he does engage his curiosity
he loiters and wonders what he should do
he's allergic to sweaty industry
he's as ponderous as a wisp of cloud

what is it a poet sees in the clouds?
to neglect a job is pomposity
in sunlit clouds there is no industry
does following the clouds make one lazy?
surely there are worthier things to do
better ways to use curiosity

we have choices with curiosity
there is a vast cosmos beyond the clouds
within a galaxy what's there to do?
who could claim a cosmic pomposity?
while plopped in a chair and being lazy
with no hint of muscular industry

(. . . continued from page 78)

a novelist may boast of industry
with a strenuous curiosity
spinning a narrative isn't lazy
how many novelists write about clouds?
they have a good case for pomposity
specifically — *what does a poet do?*

he or she fabricates — *as people do* —
they evince an eccentric industry
they may take pleasure in pomposity
ego may drive their curiosity
they gaze above — following gauzy clouds
they cannot admit to being lazy

Homer and Dante — they were not lazy
our spirits vaporize — much like the clouds
there are uses for curiosity.

A Gossipy Sestina

Our lives depend on reciprocity
which is a harmonious fact to see
sharing with others is propitious
each of us has a virtuosity
with a tendency for hypocrisy
it is good to lower expectations

are you aware of your expectations?
of the nexus of reciprocity?
of the comedy of hypocrisy?
which is a gracious gentle way to see
lying's a human virtuosity
being flexible is propitious

circumspection is most propitious
we should lightly hold our expectations
a quiet poise is virtuosity
to avoid bitter reciprocity
fiascos are such common plights to see
trouble arises from hypocrisy

we give ourselves heartfelt hypocrisy
denying our faults is propitious
as a self-nourishing habit to see
complementing daily expectations
fortifying our reciprocity
undermining our virtuosity

(. . . continued from page 80)

dissembling is virtuosity
we soothe disturbance with hypocrisy
to sidestep biting reciprocity
to stop derision is propitious
to aid societal expectations
a beneficial tradition to see

how much honesty do we safely see?
how do we measure virtuosity?
may we minimize our hypocrisy?
how should we balance our expectations?
a sense of justice is propitious
we do need lawful reciprocity

we all depend on reciprocity
justice and kindness are propitious
to counterbalance our hypocrisy.

Would it be of happy benefit to
you to be able to listen in on
the private thoughts of people as they are
talking to you to perceive the snark and
judgment instantaneously opposed
to your heartfelt opinions and to see
the welcoming expressions of faces
belie the negativity truly
animating their craniums and would
you in response be crestfallen and
crushed radiating your shame for all to
see or would you rather assume the guise
of cheerful agreement knowing in your
heart — *this is a person you don't care for?*

It seems there's a
politician
in each of us
with a touch of
hypocrisy.

My mind is bowl of vibratory
echoes and words resonate synapses
occasionally with eruptions of
emotions and then there follows a choice
of what to do and even decisions
to do nothing are responses that make
ripples with a propulsion of thoughts — *but*
there is also the happenstance of a
frog that disturbs a pond with a *plop* that
reverberates waves of water and air
and my ears absorb sound with a happy
propensity to hear enchanted with
the magic of continuous pregnant
vibes — *or I may choose to be a sourpuss.*

I am a mere
mouse inside a
maze and I am
the magician
who has made it.

A sunrise is surpassing beauteous
the sun is as wonderful as a toad
the two aren't compared ordinarily
to equate them raises befuddlement
but I'm a poet of rascality
hoping to earn your appreciation

the sun deserves our appreciation
in every season it is beauteous
the sun is the author of rascality
without the sun there wouldn't be a toad
does seeing the truth spark befuddlement?
a toad's discounted ordinarily

a toad is funny ordinarily
is it worthy of appreciation?
its existence is a befuddlement
few could say that a toad is beauteous
and link together a sunburst and toad
doing so would be a rascality

is the toad a goad of rascality?
is it a punchline ordinarily?
how often do we think about a toad?
a toad escapes our appreciation
who of us believes it is beauteous?
it may be a *prompt* of befuddlement

(. . . continued from page 84)

a toad's apart from our befuddlement
a toad is above our rascality
its quiet dignity is beauteous
it's unflappable ordinarily
a toad doesn't want appreciation
there's not a hint of pride within a toad

a mirror's irrelevant to a toad
a mirror captures *our* befuddlement
it entangles *our* appreciation
mirrors propagate *our* rascality
but we don't think so ordinarily
we believe our image is beauteous

we are enthralled by what is beauteous
we are unconscious ordinarily
and dedicated to rascality.

As a rascal with too much time on your
hands you may have found yourself enthralled by
throwing a ball against a wall to hear
The *pa-dumping* brilliance of its *bounding*
off the wall and cement and back to you
for you to catch it with a glove whereby
you extemporized the magnificence
manipulating the speed and height of
the toss amplifying the *bop* and *plop*
improvising a *bebop* and *diddly*
composing with *lazy loops* and *lopes* — and
no one told you how to do it — all you
needed was a ball a wall and a glove
and — *you became a maestro of music.*

No frog ever took
as much pleasure in
a solitary
plop.

Buddhists are attached to rituals like
ringing bells at intervals of minutes
as signals for the beginning of our
sittings of meditation but Jane is
a rascal who rings the bell without a
reason other than the joy of hearing
it which she did the other day with a
mallet so in seeking proper order
I crept behind her and pinched the bell with
my fingers which silenced the vibrations
immediately though I didn't think
through the consequences sufficiently
as Jane retained the mallet in her hand
and she spun and struck me on the forehead.

Vibrations
of sound were
replaced by
a throb of
sensation.

Our clever scientists building on the
findings of earlier scientists learned
to synchronize several telescopes
dispersed on separate continents and
thereby they use the entire Earth as a
camera to photograph a ring of
fire that signifies the circumference of
the event horizon of a black hole
so that their theories are verified and
they can see where it is that gravity
is infinite and the passage of time
is instantaneous around which a
swirl of a galaxy of stars are held
in thrall to spin perpetually fast.

Mind-bending photos
epitomize how
far we've progressed
from starving nomads —
where are we going?

I hold a sheet of paper containing
a newly composed poem up to the
light and the sun shines through it and appears
exquisite revealing the handiwork
of people in the ability to
convert a forest of trees into sheets
of paper upon which we may transmit
confabulations illuminations
of cultural inheritance and we
don't ordinarily appreciate
the details of what we do and how we
live in the million manifestations
of our habits which may be good or bad
depending on our daily perspectives.

What is ephemeral?
as I do admit to
being slightly ashamed
of how much paper I
waste.

A photon bounces around inside the
sun trillions of times in tens of thousands
of years before it reaches the surface
and is liberated speeding away
faster than anything else in every
direction to mix its transitory
flight with the light of a trillion trillion
other suns that serves to illuminate
the void of space and the small proportion
of particles that strike Earth take only
eight minutes to come touching the ice and
barren winds of the Arctic and scorching
the Sahara with fire and infusing
the air with oxygen by using trees.

Clever people use
prisms to reveal
the spectrum of
color and the
splendor of light.

The companionship of animals and
people is somewhat harmonious as
I can't imagine living without the
clever rascality of Kitcat as
he reminds me to replenish his dish
with nibbles by noisily pawing the
bag with a determined insistence and
across the street my neighbor Jeff takes the
sun on his porch along with Carter
the pooch with collar and chain restraining
his rambunctious expression and when he
sees another dog amble by he's moved
to bark vociferously only to
to hear insistently *"CARTER QUIET."*

Kitcat escaped my
house often enough
to know he'd rather
be inside so now
he's happy at the
window.

When there comes an itch
must there be a scratch?

is an itch a glitch
of the skin — a twitch
that becomes a rash?

Flighty Terza Rima

There was a roaring storm at 1 a.m.
but I didn't know it — being asleep —
for that I'm grateful — *I sincerely am* —

the wind howled and I didn't hear a peep
while the air conditioner cooled my home
my slumbering was especially deep

my dreams were weaving a heavenly dome
catastrophic thunder fractured the sky
to me it was a soothing metronome

a cataclysmic tumult passed on by
forked bolts of lightning seared the humid air
the devil's scorching spears were on the fly

the Earth did what it did — *I didn't care* —
not an echo displaced my derriere.

Sour Grapes Terza Rima

With ease my words may skip across the page
just a smidgen of my mind can do it
but writing poems doesn't earn a wage

it's propitious to display some wit
but most don't mess with poetry today
in mainstream culture my habits don't fit

on a sheet of paper I have my say
I disembowel my secrets — *and I bleed* —
within narrow margins I get my way

I'm doing my best to disperse my seeds
to consummate delight — *and to triumph* —
it's a shame that very few women read

how often is it that my dreams go poof?
is it any wonder I often spoof?

The Lombardi Trophy Sestina

America fancies Vince Lombardi
champion coach of the Green Bay Packers
that he's a god is not hyperbole
Americans don't like humility
America scorns pathetic losers
he's a cynosure of our aggression

football is ingenious aggression
we've made a fetish of Vince Lombardi
he triumphed over piteous losers
through skillful use of the Green Bay Packers
he effused a winning humility
which could be considered hyperbole

Americans revere hyperbole
all of our heroes display aggression
hiding aggression with humility
with the grinning swank of Vince Lombardi
the general of the Green Bay Packers
the team that produced our battered losers

we are petrified of being losers
that we're obsessed is not hyperbole
though we don't play for the Green Bay Packers
we rhapsodize with glitzy aggression
we look with longing to Vince Lombardi
a giant of Hollywood humility

(. . . continued from page 95)

after winning we show humility
we are grateful for confounded losers
and we celebrate like Vince Lombardi
that he's alive is not hyperbole
he inspires civilized aggression
well organized like the Green Bay Packers

we internalize the Green Bay Packers
we parade with armored humility
we pontificate humbled aggression
and depend upon persistent losers
our contentment isn't hyperbole
we love our deity Vince Lombardi

we adore the grin of Vince Lombardi
it's the fever of our hyperbole —
taint of American humility.

I adored the Minnesota Vikings
the Vikings purpled my adolescence
as they were succeeding I was winning

they spiced the flavor of my pubescence
I couldn't wait for Sunday afternoon
each victory was an incandescence

I put all of my faith in Warren Moon
he was the flashy Viking quarterback
he was going to win the Super Bowl — *soon* —

but my devotion obtained no payback
four times the Vikings lost the Super Bowl
and now I am a dipsomaniac

I could have been happy — could've been bold —
the Minnesota Vikings left me cold.

Is the heart of Zen a purposelessness?
supposedly Zen's for liberation
which is a tinkering with consciousness

there is my lustful manipulation
I always struggle to get what I want
so desires drive my expectations

I make the Zendo my favorite haunt
to seize the inexpressible and sing
I'd like to grasp enlightenment and flaunt

around the corner it comes with a zing
I attack my problems with a battle ax
to all my precious opinions I cling

I expend my energy to the max
and it's true — *I don't know how to relax.*

Ezra Pound wanted poets to invent
he wrote a book entitled *Make It New*
to give originality assent

the majesty of the ancients *he knew*
with an encyclopedia of thought
he sought a dawning millennium's view

too bad his time was so bitter and fraught
he was encumbered with frenetic passions
it's sad humanity is full of rot

it seems we're given a choice of poisons
few of us achieve ethereal peace
we are surrounded by spoliation

within our time we are *a puny piece*
the tumult of life passes without cease.

I climb the slope to Houlton on my bike
I watch my shadow attacking the hill
my blood is racing and my heartrate spikes

I perpetuate force and spin a thrill
as I want my body comely and fit
I tend toward an obsessive overkill

and then I sniff a smell that cows emit
imbibing the odor of manure
with repeated samplings I expect it

cows don't care about muscular vigor
they languidly loiter about the mud
they don't give a *moo* about their figures

they don't want exercise to rile their blood
they are in heaven — *and chewing their cud.*

Moo

—*Tekkan*

www.ingramcontent.com/pod-product-compliance
Lightning Source LLC
LaVergne TN
LVHW061625070526
838199LV00070B/6579